THE REVERSE POINT

a timeless odyssey through the mind of God

By Josh Jacob

authorHOUSE®

AuthorHouse™
1663 Liberty Drive
Bloomington, IN 47403
www.authorhouse.com
Phone: 1-800-839-8640

First published by AuthorHouse 9/1/2010

ISBN: 978-1-4520-0368-9 (sc)
ISBN: 978-1-4520-0369-6 (e)

Library of Congress Control Number: 2010904046

Printed in the United States of America

This book is printed on acid-free paper.

This book is dedicated to
my mother Ilene,
for whom I dearly love.

Just suppose there was an end to the universe, there must be a reverse point. This is the eternal existence of God as we've come to be. So let's go on a timeless odyssey and explore him.

As far as I could remember, I was probably around 5 years old when I began gazing into the stars. While doing so, I would always desperately wonder. As I matured and acquired a better comprehension of the universe, I was always overwhelmingly astounded by its very nature. From the immense proportions of its entities, such as the planets, stars and galaxies. To the vast distances between them. I'll never forget the first time I captured Saturn in my tiny refractor telescope. I think I was around 14 years old. I was completely shocked. It just appeared like this perfect little entity shining through the surrounding blackness. Like a bright new bouncing ball except with exquisite rings. The image although small, I had witnessed the grand essence of God. As I knew the universe must be infinite, by my mid twenties its very principle had become undeniably clear. There must always be a reverse point! But during that time more importantly there had become a profound will in me to write. I hope you enjoy our timeless odyssey.

Let's set out well after sunset, upon a clear moonless winter's night, far from city lights away from all light pollution. As you gaze deeply into the heavens although you could see about 1,000 stars. You're truly seeing a diminutive amount the universe actually contains. Which as a galaxy like our own Milky Way contains an average number of around 200 billion stars. It's only one of about 100 billion galaxies reaching out nearly 13.7 billion light-years to the end of the known universe. Which as this could only be the point to the infinite, as we've evolved through. We can not come to imagine not existing. Which as well throughout species it's only our consciousness that is not predominantly instinct. This must be our eternal soul, the inner presence of God. So just for a moment, try to imagine not existing.... The universe from its complex physics to very life itself, it could only be for a reason. Which if you've ever simply blew the seeds off a dandelion, as they'll eventually sprout, decompose and nourish the soil. You've truly touched God. As through the food chain we could continue perceiving God through the conscious. As although predators like cheetahs after making a kill, often will have it stolen by more powerful predators like lions or hyenas. A cheetah with its great speed almost, always will easily kill again. Which even while their speed has become inevitable, could it really be just pure evolution? Well although God's very individual existence is clearly unseen. We could as well evoke God's actuality through the domino effect. Which for the dominos to advance, there simply must always be an initial force. As naturally being provided by you, yet essentially through your nutrient energy. So just suppose there was a beginning of time. At that very exact instant there would be nothing there to counteract it. Therefore the universe could only exist by the very will of God. As we've come from God's consciousness amongst all species, only we'll have the ability to journey the universe. Which is the very defining justification of our eternal soul. As clearly in around a billion years from now as our Sun begins expanding into a red giant and its extreme heat scorches Earth. We'll have already escaped as species perish. Till now through our ever enduring ancestry as the environment has come to proceed our evolution. By their very honor we're the one's whom must carry out our destiny. So in 1994 when comet Shoemaker-Levy 9 plunged into Jupiter's atmosphere. Were we actually within the very hand of God? Well, suppose we hadn't been. The comet could've possibly collided with Earth and destroyed humankind. So was it just the chance of circumstance that Jupiter evolved within our solar system? Which throughout eons Jupiter's massive volume has been generating gravity, acting like a gigantic vacuum cleaner, attracting many of the wandering asteroids and comets that might otherwise hit Earth? As Shoemaker-Levy 9 had become the first planetary impact in recorded history, it captivated scientists all around the world.

But it raised the question of an asteroid or a comet that could be truly fated for us. Ever so humble God may have answered it. As Shoemaker-Levy 9 occurred just around the time we were beginning to develop the technology to deflect an asteroid or a comet. And while the incident persuaded the U.S. Congress to direct NASA a new search program immediately to attempt to shield ourselves. As we celebrated Shoemaker-Levy 9 we must have been duly honoring God. As indeed we actually owe our very existence to an impact. Which as the 6 mile wide asteroid that wiped out the dinosaurs 65 million years ago had evoked our evolution. By now our mind must assure us that we don't go their way. As although the dinosaurs reigned for 170 million years, yet it still hadn't come to prolong their lives. While amongst modern species, notably our destiny is relatively evident through lions, as they continuously execute themselves. Indeed this is just their instinct, which when a male lion triumphs in a battle with another male, then kills the cubs in his pride. It shortly brings the lioness into estrus for mating.

But this wasn't our evolution.

As throughout our generations as the passing of knowledge among all has become our very supremacy. Man's remarkable journey continues.

So just how exactly did God create us? By the atom of course. While they originated on Earth. As Earth evolved along with the Sun. The Sun evolved from the material of a previously deceased star. As star birth evolved throughout our galaxy, all galaxies evolved through the big bang causing the birth of the known universe. Which by the reverse point while we're actually acknowledging God through the very atoms that constitute our mind. Let's just think. As the atoms which generated an elephant's mind equally evolved through God. An elephant could not contemplate it. As although it's an extremely intelligent species as it clearly mourns its deceased. This probably really is solely grief. As without the basic understanding of the universe. Could an elephant come to even think the soul departs? Which as our very notion of God is overwhelming. His mutuality amongst us could be as well sensed through species like bear. As even while they naturally nurture their young for just several years.

However unequal as our children become independent, we'll still always deeply care for them. While they'll equally always care for us. Which our unending love perhaps could only span the soul.

But while we share 98 percent of our DNA with a chimpanzee, could we actually have been chosen? Eminently as we've evolved through our family tree as the only species to ever revolutionize the planet. Leopards exist but of course tigers don't launch rockets. Which as we inevitably stood upright, it couldn't have been the luck of fate. As God must have altered evolution for our very prospering. Which as we've come to manipulate species just like in the wild, as they obey their nutrient requirements in the hunt or the continuous journey to find food. Appropriately the natural struggle to survive is surrendered when we grant this. Which as we've domesticated species there's been pure harmony. This is of course evident in the bond between a lion and a trainer, as even savage instinct becomes tame. But could our very worldwide domination of species be truly justified? Well set aside all perceived notions of animal cruelty. Our very natural existence has already caused many species to become extinct. Which as we've been stripping their natural habitat through our development, the ever immensely growing populations also caused global warming, while even the majestic polar bears become endangered. But even while they diminish and however heartbreaking this really is. We should just try not to feel too morally dispirited. As although climate change could eventually have catastrophic effects upon us. Yet of course any advanced civilization could only have evolved through the alteration of the environment. Which as we've now come close to 7 billion of our kind inhabiting Earth. After all for ourselves and species, the human enterprise must truly be destined for other worlds. So in the meantime we're deeply attempting to justify our existence through our continued efforts of wildlife conservation and as well exploring the most efficient fuel. But nevertheless amidst the world's apparent ever increasing chaos. Have you ever simply gazed into a chimp's eyes and clearly sensed yours and even Man's insignificance? Well you still must be just only acknowledging God, as our vision has come to establish. But just where exactly is God? While he seems to have granted us a hint through natural beauty. As we've all seen sunshine brilliantly dispersing through the clouds, or a perfect sunset which appear so beautiful as if they've come from Heaven. As in a near death experience when someone clinically dies, yet survives swearing having seen a bright shining light. Even while viewing sunlight glistening across a lake we're seeing God's essence that the soul perhaps experiences near death. Whereas light must fundamentally exist, our eyes could only be windows to the soul. So assuming heaven exists, just why did God create the physical universe? Well amongst God's actual known justification there must be defining logic. As of course there's clear evidence that life evolves through time.

As suppose the universe was finite, or had been created essentially without God. Although this is obviously impossible. But amidst the life evoking existence of asteroids and comets. Instead of the Earth being impacted by an object about 7 miles in diameter on average every 100 million years.

It would be struck suppose once every 500 years.

As of course without God's very consciousness, 65 million years ago today we amid the greater mammals would never have evolved. So while we have and know that there's cataclysms still inevitable such as the Sun's expansion and the colossal collision between the

Milky Way and our neighboring galaxy Andromeda. As both don't start up for around 1 and 5 billion years. By then our technology should clearly allow us to survive.

Which today when we gaze into the heavens, although God's unseen. We could sense our time between him. As well descending all around us through the natural constitute of life. Even while trees and plants are unconscious. As they've come to make the Earth habitable for all.

This is God ever-present. But although we're only able to detect the universe reaching out 13.7 billion light-years to the big bang.

As it created all the matter within the known universe including our mind.

Just imagine that relatively the known universe would be the equivalent size of an atom. Which think of the known universe to be a cube, and how large an infinite number of cubes would be stacked upon it. Only through God we easily could. As naturally upon the Earth, remarkably we could as well see the clouds deeply resemble universal nebula, the great pillars of creation.

While amidst the clouds on a pleasantly warm spring afternoon as a gentle breeze passes by.

If your emotions have ever evoked such a

natural presence while carefully watching a clock. Indeed God's essential motion has profoundly influenced us since the sunrise awoke primeval Man. Eons later Neanderthals hunted by daylight. And as civilization had begun, modern humans had taken to the sea. By nightfall guided by the stars we voyaged the globe. So through time as we've come destined to prevail. Before long we'll greatly have to. Which as the Earth orbits the Sun in an ellipse that gradually changes shape over time, the tilt of the Earth towards the Sun also changes. As the interaction of these changes flip the climate from warm to cold. We'll be plunged into another global ice age within 30,000 years, with freezing temperatures lasting perhaps 100,000 years. But while the conditions will be tragic, will it even matter? As I think perhaps within 1,000 years from now we'll have already begun colonizing the other habitable worlds within our galaxy and even in one's beyond. But during that time however of course in a sense we could never do so. As after all traveling through space-time takes time. Which clearly in 1,000 years just while setting out to the nearest stars at let's say 50 light-years distant. Even if we're able to travel a fraction of the speed of light at 10 million m.p.h. It would take us over 3,000 years. Which assume the nearest world is further throughout the 100,000 light-years of the Milky Way. Although throughout the generations we would eventually get there. The enterprise would've become our world. But nevertheless just imagine what our technology will be like in 1,000 years. And then think of what technology was like 1,000 years ago. It's through the imagination that our quantum leaps should eventually allow us to easily overcome time. As assume by the next millennium we'll have discovered wormholes (Theoretical shortcuts connecting two regions of space-time distant from each other).

As well if God had initially set the Earth's orbit off, it would be simply too close or too far from the Sun for us to have evolved and even begun sensing wormholes. As after all even while Man had designed the clock. Indeed it was the very hand of time that were its true creator. As although wormholes are still theoretical, it's because they remain in deep harmony with eternal possibility. Which clearly as we're allegedly amongst several very elusive phenomena. Eminently e.t. big-foot, the lockness monster and ghosts. As they're unexplained, there is indeed one notion in which they're completely exposed.

It's the reverse point. As surely some civilization has evolved. While they're simply somewhere beyond, whereas big-foot and the

lockness monster of course remain evolutionary concepts. Assume ghosts are amongst us.
They still must exist, so should we really fear
them? As within God's existence after all, he's
truly all and whom we've come to know.

While the view of the stars is quite majestic
and sunrise continues warming the sky. The
very existence above our atmosphere is unin-
habitable.

Which as life has evolved to thrive here
upon Earth, Gods truly freed us. As his natural freedom could come to be clearly sensed
within our labor demanding society.

So of course the greatest way to search out

our innermost freedom, is profoundly harmonizing with God.

Which at the ocean's horizon as the gorgeous sunset tranquilizes the sky. Within God's honor our prison system preserves freedom simply by taking it away. As it's truly a gift being beneath the stars.

I would like to wholly dedicate this to all whom unrighteously lost their freedom. Notably the Jews of the Nazi concentration camps and the African-American slaves. Shall their souls forever be, for they were born free they shall remain free.

God's essential freedom is eminent at the Earth's poles. As even where there's devastating cold, yet species like the polar bear and the penguin have evolved to prosper. However as we're still likely the only species whom appreciates God. Even our relative the chimpanzee perhaps sees the stars as just some really out of the reach fruit. Which amongst all whomever gazed into the stars and wondered. By the very recognition of God, I would just like a moment to acknowledge some of the most brilliant minds whom came to be. Eminently our Founding Fathers of astronomy. Galileo Galilei, Isaac Newton, and Albert Einstein. I would like to say more about them, but while they're out of my era, what I could say is that while they've paved the way to today's minds, our love and enthusiasm for the stars just continues.

To Mr. Carl Sagan. What you have given us could only have come from God. You've enlightened all. Shall your soul forever be. To Mr. Stephen Hawking. Though you shall remain physically restricted, you're able to move mountains with your mind. I couldn't forget you Mr. David Levy. Just continue aiming that telescope, as we're hoping you'll shield us from the big one.

As the very alteration of the environment has evolved our technological supremacy. Naturally we're the only species whom ever created fire. Which by far the only way even a superior class such as an orangutan could do so, would be to pass him a match. But although by now here on Earth we're clearly living our supremacy.

We must simply realize our journey to the moon which took the Apollo spacecraft just 3 days to reach. If we had continued at that pace only to the nearest star Proxima Centauri it would take us over 900,000 years. Likely however such a trip will only be taken through statistics. But God's truth is truly everlasting. As even when the voyager spacecraft left the solar system at 37,000 m.p.h. At that speed it would still take voyager 80,000 years to reach proxima Centauri. And of course far beyond that our neighboring galaxy Andromeda is more than 2 million light-years away. While there's billions upon billions of other galaxies that get ever more distant. But as we've come to solve the world, and today know theoretically that through a wormhole we could easily travel through the vastness of space. One day will it actually be our great privilege to go beyond the faraway universe and at last be acknowledged by God? Although this is truly an appropriate notion, as the infinite remains nevertheless yet just suppose we did! Where would God himself, the very pure utter being ever begin ending?? But as we've come to exist however, naturally through time perhaps one day in heaven our soul will. Which even while lights evolved traveling the mind-boggling speed of 186,000 m.p.s. The sun actually shines from around 8 minutes ago, while the nearest stars are seen back for decades. Which as we're already enveloped by God's heavenly essence.

The known universe reaching out 13.7 billion light-years is truly an eternity.

And until recently the time before the big bang was seen as a dark lifeless void. But remarkably a theoretical proposition perceives the infinite is full of creation. What this means is that the big bang is constant throughout the universe. Which through big bangs exists an

infinite number of parallel universes compris-
ing an entire multiverse. While clearly intelligent life must inhabit at least one of these
quantums. As they're just so faraway. Imag-
inable too within the known universe alone
there must be at least some others, as it still
contains more stars than the stars. Which
when gazing into just only the nearest one's.
Have you ever flipped through one of those
little motion picture books? Well imagine the
starry sky of Earth as one of those drawings,
being a point in the universe, proceeding as a
moment of time. Which in this little book of
course there would be no final picture.

While our mind's so clearly blessed our

carnal grant has become overshadowed. But along with our exceptional dexterity and adequate strength, we've truly come to be the most efficient species ever. So one day at the very touch of a hand, when we at last manipulate the controls upon our initial star ship. Just equally acknowledge the accomplishment of an Olympic gymnast. Which otherwise as many species will always be the most supreme athletes. In pure comparison while a cheetah could sprint to 70 m.p.h. and some of us could weight train 300 Lbs. Amongst our mind we're right there with them.

So just how profound was our carnal grant? Eminently our cousins the Neanderthals with their burly physique, had such crushing strength. Along with a thrusting spear they hunted large animals like red deer, horse and wild cattle in the forest in ambush. About 45,000 years ago however, the climate of Europe went through a burst of very sudden switches between warm and cold that would've transformed the Neanderthals environment. The forest on which they depended began to recede, giving way to open plains. On these plains the Neanderthals thrusting spear and ambush strategy wouldn't have worked. About 30,000 years ago however as modern humans spread into Europe, they made lighter stone points that could be fitted onto lighter spear shafts. As well with their less stocky build and greater agility, these could be thrown enabling our ancestors to hunt more effectively in the open landscape. But while the very disappearance of the Neanderthals has yet to be completely determined. Our creation of the javelin just had to be destined. As we could still actually see the very essential structure of our technological enterprise.

Well after sunset on a clear moonless late fall or early winter's night away from light pollution. Look almost directly overhead for the W shaped constellation Cassiopeia. With binoculars scan the area of the sky out a little ways from the highest pointer. You'll notice a faint stretched patch of light. This is billions of stars radiating from the bright dense core of the Andromeda galaxy. What you're actually seeing is gravity inevitably pulling Andromeda towards us.

But even traveling at 270,000 m.p.h. we know Andromeda won't collide with our galaxy for around 5 billion years. But when it does as gravity tugs on each others stars. The two galaxies will become utterly distorted. But through gravity as Andromeda and the Milky Way will eventually convene. Galaxies evolve through this process. And with all their creations such as black holes, pulsars, quasars and planets conceivably teeming with diverse life-forms.

A galaxy comes through the very pith of possibility, which our technology could only have come to naturally advance by. So rightfully by the javelin, this is equally evident through the automobile, aircraft and space shuttle, as they evolved neutralizing gravity. So while it's been daunting to establish an efficient fuel, we assume e.t must have. As through their deep evolutionary advancement in which they've exhausted technology. They're evidently not traversing space on gasoline. But nevertheless amidst our latest undertakings in spacecraft propulsion, and the ultra concept of wormholes. For over a century as the automobiles evolved, we've clearly seen the extent of possibility. Which today relative to technological quantum leaps, even the long imagined skycar will eventually take to the sky. So just sometime in the future however distant, a real formidable starship must be upon us. And when we at last reach the stars should we make contact with a supreme civilization, will there be harmony among worlds? Well as we assume advanced intelligence will have figured out how to. Just somewhere throughout time, however often intelligent life may creep in, and how very divergent they will have become. Naturally by being able to utilize the vast amounts of matter and space within the universe. As their species grow and colonize throughout and amongst the galaxies. The alleged supercivilizations might even come to interconnect. Which as this of course remains speculation. Whereas a recently advancing civilization like our own. Even while the populations ever increasing, as we're strictly limited for now, conceivably such harmony couldn't be. So wars are fought! But clearly as our soldiers perish in honor. Just perhaps throughout the eternities, all the young civilizations endured wars. As after all such extreme competition is as well a very heart of evolution. But nevertheless if we are indeed the only intelligent species out there in the universe amongst the countless trillions of stars. One shall come to simply ask the question why?

Otherwise the very concept of God has become controversial, because through him exists within us extremely severe iniquity. But as we've come to contemplate the inhuman acts of murder, child abuse, animal cruelty and feel the hate. Suppose everything had evolved only through a mere instant. It would hold the ability to justify all! As from God I would like a due moment to speak through hate for justice for all. As earlier on as humans like the Neanderthals survived by the utter exploitation of animals. Amongst today's technology simply butchering them just for their fur is certainly expendable.

But if however the only way that humans could ever truly unite, is actually utilizing the stars. The justification of course already exists. As through our consequence as the computer commands countless information into its own virtual existence. It's simple logic the computers originated to actually evoke God's mind. So after all whereas computability has been destined for us to persist the eternally sound universe. No matter how advanced we or any universal entity will have become will its intelligence ever be able to create it.

As God's mind will simply always be. Which ever so appropriately indeed Albert Einstein once said "I have no special talents I am only passionately curious." So just through my curiosity I will assume that amongst the possibility of e.t and their supreme capabilities. As they've yet to invade us God's righteousness is truly an element. As although it's unseen, it's our very belief in God guiding us through life when situations seem bleak or even impossible. Which just suppose God effortlessly granted us our lives. Would there be dreams? As there always will be, it's truly God whom we've come to desire. Which as we're clearly justified. Have you ever slipped on an icy surface in the wintertime and thank God you didn't fall? It just happens! But did God just happen?

As this is truly the eternal question naturally irony doesn't exist. Which as God will always be the final frontier, it's his very inescapable consciousness that overshadows his discreetness. So no matter what just continue gazing into the stars. But ultimately as Gods ordained them as we've come to be. Should we really believe there's a special reason for us?

As the enchanting split among our ape ancestors will always be eminent. Science has established that human evolution is fundamentally indistinguishable to all evolved life. So instead of being chosen by God, we're perceived as merely the ape whom got lucky! As this is duly acknowledged of course Man's evolution wasn't blessed a magic wand. As our evolution was surely a very long arduous journey. But as we now hold the inaugural blueprints to eventually colonize Mars, our reasons crystal-clear.

What makes this so daunting to recognize within our individual lives is the overwhelming existence of destiny, as there's now close to 7 billion people living through God. But whereas our significance has become justly dissolved. Just suppose you were the only entity within the entire universe. Your existence would seem utterly destined.

As in 1994 when comet shoemaker-Levy 9 plunged into Jupiter's atmosphere, were we actually within the very hand of God? Well as we know that chaotic events are inevitably linked through God. Throughout eons within our solar system Jupiter's neutralization of gravity between incoming asteroids and comets, has granted the Earth a planet which is able to generate life a chance to evolve it. But after all 65 million years ago an asteroid ended the reign of the dinosaurs. Which even while it had evoked our evolution, we must acknowledge that one day an asteroid or a comet will strike again! But just as it's headed towards us, assume we deflect it.

We must have achieved our destiny, as we begin our reign as true masters of the universe. Which as our faith remains. Throughout our odyssey as I unraveled the very intricacies of the reverse point, when I ultimately sensed God it was truly a breathtaking experience and an honor to compose. Indeed God's just a notion, but while it's as far as the mind could reach it reveals a legacy amongst him, which is an understanding to forever cherish. It's been my great privilege and I sincerely thank you for granting me the opportunity to share God. Good night, God bless us.

www.ingramcontent.com/pod-product-compliance
Lightning Source LLC
Chambersburg PA
CBHW050341290526
45785CB00006B/2589